WONDERING

WONDERING

Feelings, Emotions
and Building Resilience

BOB VOGEL

A WRITERS MATTER INITIATIVE
WWW.WRITERSMATTER.ORG

Charleston, SC
www.PalmettoPublishing.com

Wondering
Feelings, Emotions and Building Resilience

First Edition

Paperback ISBN: 979-8-8229-1590-9

DEDICATION

This book is dedicated to the most important people in my life. To my wife Marlyn, my sons Jon and Dan, my daughters-in-law Kate and Katie and my three very special granddaughters, Anya, Tally and Mabel.

To all of the children, artists and teachers who contributed to this book and shared their spirit of Wondering.

BY ALEJANDRA JIMENEZ

**It is a happiness to wonder;
it is a happiness to dream.**

—EDGAR ALLAN POE

ACKNOWLEDGEMENTS

STUDENT VOICES – FAMILY AND FRIENDS

Anya Vogel
Noah Poolman
Lucas Mitchell Gordon

Tally Vogel
Nate Poolman

Mabel Dunphy Vogel
Jacob Milo Gordon

STUDENT VOICES – SCHOOL DISTRICT OF PHILADELPHIA

Gus Anderson
Noah Deneke
Mirabelle McNair-Boyle
Liam Petit Frere
Juno Stevenson
Nur-Jennah Rivera
Tahid Horton

Benjamin Barnes
Nora Fussaro
Brighton Norton
Cora Schofield
Katherine Wikander
Jordyn Dumas

Imani Crawford
Maggie Marcus-Carlin
Jasper O'Neill
Ayden Shannon
Nova Wilson-Ruff
Simone Harris

Jessica Tellez Hernandez
Erin Jordan
Jayden Troiano
Autumn L. Clarke
Yeimi Reyes
Jose Saloma
Mariel Duran
Jael Martinez

Cavin Dani
Linda Zuniga Hernandez
Emoni Huertas
London Jordan
Jael Martinez
Louie Verrecchio
Andrea Valera

Jiayuan Chen
Andrea Valera
Zora Heard
Alicia Rivera-Latimer
Jasim Smith
Cristobalina Rosales
Suri Juarez

Juliette Alvarez
Janaliz Bourdierd
Elser Pop Caal
Aaron Ruan
Anna Wu

Safiatou Balde
Dontae Brown
Sabiha Rahman
Jeanette Tucker
Eric Zhang

Genevieve Bonar
Minglang Chen
Darien Rai-Khoeun
Miley Wiggins

STUDENT ARTISTS

Juliette Alvarez	Genevieve Bonar	Minglang Chen
Sabiha Rahman	Anna Wu	Allayah Drain
Jayvin Mendez	Noah Poolman	Khadija Rouine
Makaiyah Uqdah	Sahara Jackson	Alejandra Jimenez
Nam Nguyen	Emoni Huertas	Zora Heard Color

STUDENT ARTISTS - SPECIAL ACKNOWLEDGEMENTS

Leslie Pugach	Writing Consultant and Editor
Marylyn Vogel, Ed.D. ABSN, Licensed Psychologist	Content Consultant
Blair Pomerantz MSS, LCSW, Clinical Social Worker/Therapist	Consulting Teacher
Carl Jackson, C.W. Henry School, Philadelphia	Consulting Teacher
Kelly Ann Coughlin, J.H. Moore School, Philadelphia	Consulting Teacher/Art Coordinator
Joan Carter Williams, E. M. Stanton School, Philadelphia	Consulting Teacher
Anne Olvera, E.M. Stanton Philadelphia	Consulting Teacher
Emily Kocotis, J.H. Moore School, Philadelphia	Consulting Art Teacher

All royalties from the sale of this book will support
Writers Matter educational programs.

ABOUT THE AUTHOR

Bob Vogel, Ed.D. recently retired from full-time teaching after 43 years at La Salle University in the Department of Education and currently serves as Professor Emeritus of Education. He taught in public schools for three years before earning a doctorate in Educational Psychology and Organizational Development from Temple University.

In 2005, Bob became the Founding Director of Writers Matter (a 501C3 -nonprofit). The central mission of this program is to provide a unique and innovative opportunity for students in grades 2-8 to learn critical writing skills through personal journal writing, by creating the opportunity to write about their lives at a time when expressing personal ideas and having their voices heard is so important. Writers Matter offers research-based strategies which motivate students to write, work diligently to improve their writing skills and to think more critically about the world. Since its inception, Writers Matter has served over 26,000 students. During the 2022-2023 school year, the Writers Matter program is implemented in 18 schools in the Philadelphia metropolitan area and includes over 75 teachers and 3000 students. For more specific information about Writers Matter access writersmatter.org.

Bob lives in the Art Museum neighborhood of Philadelphia with his wife Marlyn. They appreciate exploring the richness of city life. He also enjoys opportunities for adventure travel, biking, hiking and summers at the Jersey shore. Spending time getting together with his two sons Jon and Dan, their wives Kate and Katie, and his three granddaughters Anya, Tally and Mabel is a priority. And yes, all his granddaughters participated in *Wondering*, the genesis of which came from a casual conversation with a granddaughter that any grandparent can appreciate!

Bob has co-authored numerous articles and several books including *Methods of Teaching: Applying Cognitive Science to Promote Student*

*Learning (*Feden & Vogel) - McGraw-Hill, 2006; *Voices of Teens: Writers Matter* (Vogel & Galbraith). National Middle School Association, 2008; *Empowering Young Writers: The Writers Matter Approach* (Yost, Vogel and Lewinski). Temple University Press, 2014; Writers Matter: Empowering Voices of Israeli and Palestinian Teens -Cultural Narrative Building through Writing (Vogel & Adwan). 2016 and *Society Unmasked: Voices of Teachers and Students in Unprecedented Time* (Lewinski, McLaurin, and Vogel). Writers Matter, 2021.

TABLE OF CONTENTS

INTRODUCTION

Wondering: Feelings, Emotions and Building Resilience is about the personal reflections of children ages 8-14 who are curious, imaginative, compassionate, and vulnerable as they strive to understand themselves and those around them. As they navigate an ever-changing and complex world, they struggle with a myriad of challenging emotions and feelings. These feelings and emotions are intertwined with relationships they have with friends, parents, and family members. Letting their voices be heard and talking about what they've had to say is critical in improving their understanding of themselves and others. Children in this age group often keep many of their feelings and emotions locked up inside; they seldom have opportunities to freely discuss what they are thinking and feeling. *Wondering* provides a pathway for them to hear their inner voices. Finding concrete ways for children to take responsibility for resolving personal challenges leads to a sense of empowerment and helps build resilience and self-esteem.

You do not need to remind any parent or teacher of pre-adolescent and adolescent children how complicated it can be to understand children during this developmental stage. They are experiencing many physical, cognitive, and emotional changes which lead to frustration, difficulty making good decisions and struggles in managing relationships. *Wondering* provides opportunities for adolescents and pre-adolescents to explore these challenges both alone and with others, providing a pathway to effectively navigate life's complex issues.

Wondering is a collection of 100 "I Wonder Questions" suggested by approximately 90 students, ages 8 to 14. These "I Wonder Why" questions engage children in discussing issues that are important to them and in seeking some answers to these questions independently. Students' and teachers' responses to these questions were organized into nine categories: Understanding

Yourself; Emotions and Feelings; Fears, Anxiety and Becoming Resilient and Self-Confident, Understanding Others; Understanding Friends and Building Friendships; Family Relationships; Connecting With Your Parents and Other Adults in Your Life; Equity, Personal Responsibility and Making The World a Better Place; and Hopes and Dreams.

Wondering is more than a book to just read with a young person. It is an interactive experience which encourages adolescent and pre-adolescent children to be imaginative and reflective, as they assume responsibility for independently examining personal issues that are important to them. Reading and using *Wondering* can show a child that listening to your inner voice can be empowering.

SUGGESTIONS FOR USING THE BOOK

Wondering is designed to be an interactive experience and encourages all readers to use their imaginations and to think deeply. Begin your journey with Chapter One or wander the chapters in any order that interests you the most.

Each Chapter begins with **"I Wonder Why"** questions. Look at the questions and decide which ones are most important to you. Choose one, two or all of them to think about.

Once you feel comfortable with the questions which begin each chapter, turn the page and look at how students have responded. Their responses with be in **BLUE**.

Next, read how teachers have responded to the questions. Teachers' responses will be in **FUCHSIA**.

In the middle of each chapter, you will find a section called "Time to Wonder". This section is action oriented and provides an opportunity to use your imagination and further expand your thinking. This section has three parts:

1. More questions to "Wonder" about and further elaborate your ideas.
2. A place to write down your thoughts and ideas.
3. A place to "Doodle" your thoughts and ideas. Let your inner artist take over.

At the end of each chapter, you will find a section called "Your Turn". Here you are totally on your own. Look back at some of the questions and write down the advice you would give yourself or maybe advice you would give to others. You may want to consider this section as your personal journal.

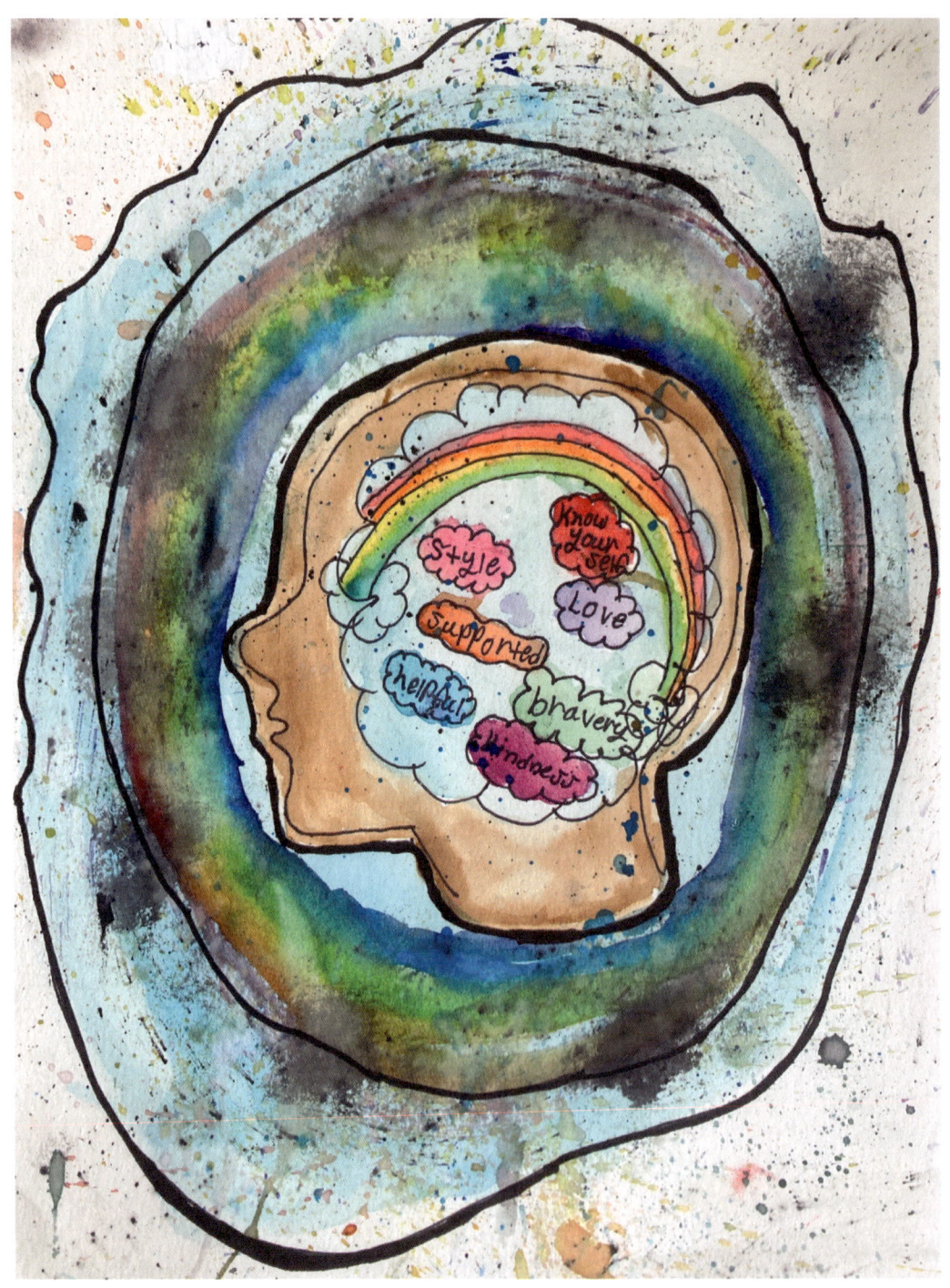

BY ALLAYAH DRAIN

CHAPTER ONE
UNDERSTANDING YOURSELF

I WONDER WHY SHARING MY FEELINGS WITH OTHERS MAKES ME FEEL GOOD.

I WONDER WHY IT IS SO DIFFICULT TO BE PROUD OF YOURSELF.

I WONDER WHY IT IS SO IMPORTANT TO ME THAT OTHERS UNDERSTAND ME.

I WONDER IF THERE IS A DIFFERENCE BETWEEN BEING ALONE AND BEING LONELY?

I WONDER WHY SHARING MY FEELINGS WITH OTHERS MAKES ME FEEL GOOD.

Because instead of keeping things inside my mind and heart, it feels better to share my feelings.

Because I feel really good when I have people I can talk to. I need others to trust and who care about me.

When you share your feelings with others, it makes you feel good because it helps you get things off your chest. If you talk to a therapist or even just a friend, it makes you feel better. Getting your emotions and feelings out so they don't build up lets you breathe.

I WONDER WHY IT IS SO DIFFICULT TO BE PROUD OF YOURSELF.

It's so difficult because you see other people doing better than you and so you compare yourself to them and that makes you feel less proud about yourself.

Because you are not sure what you are doing is really a good thing or even if others really appreciate what you have done is that good. You need to think more positively about your accomplishments and understand your strengths and weaknesses.

Because you strive so hard to achieve in life when we are recognized for doing good, we think we could have done better. You need to become more confident in yourself and think what you are accomplishing is something to be proud.

I WONDER WHY IT IS SO IMPORTANT TO ME THAT OTHERS UNDERSTAND ME.

You want to be acknowledged by others and know they care about you. This makes you feel safer in life and helps you care about others more. This makes you feel good and more worthwhile.

I WONDER IF THERE IS A DIFFERENCE BETWEEN BEING ALONE AND BEING LONELY?

There is a big difference between being alone and being lonely. Being alone is having people in your life but wanting to have your own space. Being lonely is having nobody in your life and wishing you did. I much prefer to be alone at times.

Yes, there is a difference. Being alone can be peaceful and quiet. It can make you feel independent and strong. Sometimes it is nice to be alone with your ideas or doing something that you like to do. You might feel lonely if you wanted company, but no one was around to be with you. If you feel lonely, reach out to a friend or family member and see if someone has time to spend with you, even just for a little while.

Being alone is the absence of people...it means there is no one else physically nearby. Being lonely is something you could feel even when sitting in a room full of people where you don't feel connected, understood, or supported.

BY ANONYMOUS

3

 # TIME TO WONDER

I WONDER WHY IT IS SO HARD TO BE KIND.

Saying mean jokes or being mean to be funny can be funny, but not to everyone. They might take it to heart too much. Try saying nice things to people as practice for being a kinder person.

WRITE YOUR THOUGHTS

DOODLE YOUR THOUGHTS

I WONDER WHY I GET JEALOUS OF OTHERS.

I WONDER WHY I DO NOT TRUST OTHERS.

I WONDER IF DIFFICULT TIMES MAKE US STRONGER.

I WONDER WHY IT IS OFTEN SO MUCH HARDER TO BE POSITIVE THAN NEGATIVE.

I WONDER WHY I AM SOMETIMES UNKIND TO OTHERS.

I WONDER WHY I GET JEALOUS OF OTHERS.

Feeling jealous is a feeling that you want what others have. It could be friends, athletic ability, personality, or even physical objects. You want them because you want to be more like them.

You might feel jealous if someone has something that you want or gets to do something that you want to do. It is fine to feel jealous, but maybe you can be happy for someone at the same time. That can be hard to do, but it might make you feel better to be glad for your friend!

I WONDER WHY I DO NOT TRUST OTHERS.

I have trouble trusting friends because they sometimes see that I need support, but it seems I am disappointed by what happens most of the time.

Trust takes time to build. Sometimes you need to be certain that you can trust someone and maybe you need proof that the person is trustworthy. Don't rush it. Let people show you that they are worth your trust. Remember, though, that you need to be trustworthy too.

I WONDER IF DIFFICULT TIMES MAKE US STRONGER.

One of my favorite quotes is: "Life is full of knock downs. It's how you get back up that helps build character". A difficult time is a "knock down". It's up to you whether you are going to stay down or learn from it, get back up, and keep it moving!

I WONDER WHY IT IS OFTEN SO MUCH HARDER TO BE POSITIVE THAN NEGATIVE.

Because it is hard to say nice things to others. You think you are funny, but you are usually not kind. You need to stay positive.

I think people cannot handle their negativity. Trying to deal with your negative thoughts is overwhelming. Others tend to gravitate more to negativity. The saying "misery loves company" usually holds true. Once a person hears negativity then it spreads quickly. Then, everyone starts sharing their negativity. Trying to be positive is hard, but it feels better.

This is tough. It is easier to "go low" and sometimes it feels good to say something mean or to complain. Sometimes you must get something off your chest and complain. But being negative is never productive and you usually feel bad afterwards. Try to change your thinking about how you can be helpful, kind and positive.

I WONDER WHY I AM SOMETIMES UNKIND TO OTHERS.

Being unkind might start as a funny joke to some but to others it may not be so funny, You could be hurting others and you need to be aware of the things you say before you say it. You don't want to feel bad after you were not kind to another person.

Maybe you are being unkind because you don't want to acknowledge and accept your own weaknesses and imperfections. Stick to the Golden Rule; treat others the way you want to be treated!

YOUR TURN

> I wonder why I sometimes do not like myself.
> I wonder if my friends are talking about me behind my back.

YOUR TURN

I wonder If I am going to be successful.
I wonder if difficult times make us stronger.

BY ANNA WU

10

CHAPTER TWO
EMOTIONS AND FEELINGS

I WONDER WHY IT SOMETIMES FEELS BETTER TO SHARE YOUR EMOTIONS WITH OTHERS.

I WONDER WHY EMOTIONS HAPPEN.

I WONDER WHY LIFE MUST BE SO HARD.

I WONDER WHY I LIKE TO LOCK AWAY MY PAIN.

I WONDER WHY iT SOMETiMES FEELS BETTER To SHARE YOUR EMOTiONS WiTH oTHERS.

I think it feels good to share your emotions because then someone else knows how you feel and think. They can help you feel better about yourself. Sometimes others can really help you and you might just need someone to listen to you.

Friends and family can help you feel better especially if you are feeling bad and have negative emotions.

When you realize that someone else is experiencing the same thing that you are, you often feel close to that person. When you share a problem with someone, it feels like that person is taking some of the weight off your shoulders. It is especially nice when you can do that for someone else too. It can make you feel good.

I think it feels better to share your emotions, thoughts, and challenges with others because it doesn't feel good to hold them inside you. You do not feel angry, upset, or getting ready to explode when you let your emotions out. They might know how to solve your problem or make you feel better about something.

I WONDER WHY EMoTiONS HAPPEN.

It seems emotions are a way your mind allows you to show others your real self.

Emotions mean we are human. It is natural for our minds and bodies to react to things that happen. Try not to be afraid to show your emotions – you will feel much better. I promise.

I WONDER WHY LIFE MUST BE SO HARD.

Too often life is too challenging and I feel that things seem impossible. Life is hard because it makes you do a lot of things you don't want to do.

There are so many real-life challenges that we all have to face everyday, which makes life hard sometimes.

Too often other people make your life hard for you.

I guess life is hard because God sends us obstacles all the time that we must hurdle. People make things hard for you and the world can be a cruel place to live.

Life is hard because to get things that you want or need comes with challenges to overcome. Some things are not easy. If you want to be successful, you must accept life challenges.

Poverty, grief and loss, trauma, sickness, mental health disorders, inequality, racism, sexism, homophobia...it's all so hard to manage.

I WONDER WHY I LIKE TO LOCK AWAY MY PAIN.

We like to lock away our pains because feeling pain doesn't feel good at all.

I like to lock away my pain so I don't interfere with anyone else's pain.

By locking away my pain, I don't want people to worry about me.

You might like to lock away your pain because you have this feeling of not wanting to burden others even if everybody else burdens you so much.

 # TIME TO WONDER

WONDER WHY IT IS SO HARD TO BREAK OUT OF MY SADNESS.

You have a hard time being happy after experiencing sad situations or maybe it's not always easy to get over something.

Sometimes sadness can feel like a heavy blanket you can't get out of. Try thinking about other things or surrounding yourself with things you can focus on other than the negative.

WRITE YOUR THOUGHTS

DOODLE YOUR THOUGHTS

I WONDER WHY BEING ON THE BEACH, SAND AND SEEING THE WAVES CALM ME DOWN?

I WONDER WHY SOMETIMES IT FEELS GOOD TO CRY AND OTHER TIMES IT DOESN'T.

I WONDER WHY I GET FRUSTRATED WHEN I GET AN ANSWER WRONG.

I WONDER WHY BEING ON THE BEACH, SAND AND SEEING THE WAVES CALM ME DOWN?

The beach, sand, and waves calm me down because it just sounds so soothing. It just makes my ears calm too and relaxes me.

It's the sound of the waves crashing against the shore and rolling across the sand. It's the smell of the ocean and the feel of the sea breeze. It's standing on the shoreline looking out at the vast ocean and realizing how small you really are.

The ocean and the beach help you calm down because it clears your mind, creating a sense of calm; you feel peaceful. It makes you concentrate on your breathing and helps you not think about school and homework.

There's nothing better than the beauty of nature and its repetitive sounds and smells to put a person at ease.

Seeing this view and its beauty makes me feel and realize there is SOMETHING larger in my life out there. It captivates you. You feel the beauty as it surrounds and protects you. It's surreal.

Being at the beach engages all five of your senses in a pleasing and calming way. The sound of the waves crashing calms the mind. The sand sifting through your fingers and toes is relaxing. The feel of cold ocean water on a hot sunny day is refreshing. The smell of the sea air mixed with sunblock is the perfect combination of salty and sweet. The sight of the water going on forever creates a sense of endless possibilities.

BY SAHARA JACKSON

16

I WONDER WHY SOMETIMES IT FEELS GOOD TO CRY AND OTHER TIMES IT DOESN'T.

Sometimes it feels good to cry because sometimes you are keeping in your emotions and then it feels good; sometimes you cry because something negative happened and it makes you feel sad. That can feel good too because it lets out your emotions.

People cry when they are sad, angry, frustrated, and even happy! It is a release of emotion and it feels good to let it out. Happiness and sadness are two of the strongest emotions that we have. When we cry out of sadness or frustration, it doesn't always feel good. However, that emotion DOES need to be let out and once you deal with the bad feelings, you will feel better.

I WONDER WHY I GET FRUSTRATED WHEN I GET AN ANSWER WRONG.

People feel like they need to be the best and get everything right.

You probably don't like feeling embarrassed when you get an answer wrong in front of others. If you are working on something alone, you may feel like you are not smart enough. Asking for help is a good plan.

You probably don't like feeling embarrassed when you get the answer wrong in front of others. If you are working on something alone, you may feel like you are not smart enough. Asking for help is a good thing!

BY NOAH POOLMAN

I WONDER IF KEEPING SECRETS IS A GOOD IDEA?

I WONDER WHY I AM SAD SO OFTEN.

I WONDER WHY IT HURTS SO MUCH WHEN I AM SAD.

I WONDER IF KEEPING SECRETS IS A GOOD IDEA?

It's not a good idea to keep secrets because you feel like you're putting a lot of stress in your brain. Secrets usually come out anyway, so why bother.

Keeping secrets is good because it shows that my friends can count on me to keep secrets safe. It is hard to do and most of the time the person who told me to keep a secret lets it out himself.

Keeping secrets is not a great idea. It also depends on the type of secret. No matter what your secret is, it's never a good idea to hide it from your friends. Secrets usually find a way of escaping. Once they do, they will be used against you no matter what you do.

I WONDER WHY I AM SAD SO OFTEN.

When people always body shame me, it makes me very, very sad.

Sometimes when you're sad, you need your own space and need to distance yourself from people. You should embrace these moments when you need to break away. Everyone needs their own space.

I WONDER WHY iT HURTS So MUCH WHEN I AM SAD.

When you are really sad about something, your whole body hurts, inside and outside. These are your emotions working on your brain and pushing away things that make you happier. Try talking a walk or doing something physical to get your brain to let go of what hurts you. You can also talk to someone like a friend or a parent who knows how to help you when you are so very sad.

Very few people can sit in discomfort and be comfortable.

Because it just does! There is no way around it. The things that bring sadness hurt. Death of a loved one or a pet, disappointments, and even when we feel empathy for others, all can bring on these feelings. The important thing is to talk about it with someone or even better, write about it in your Writers Matter journal. If your sadness doesn't seem to be going away, be sure that you let a trusted adult know how you are feeling so that that person can get you the help that you might need.

BY ANONYMOUS

21

YOUR TURN

YOUR TURN

BY MINGLANG CHEN

CHAPTER THREE
FEARS, ANXIETY, AND BECOMING RESILIENT AND SELF-CONFIDENT

I WONDER WHY I FEEL I ALWAYS NEED TO BE THE BEST.

I WONDER WHY I SOMETIMES DON'T LIKE MYSELF.

I WONDER WHY I FEEL I ALWAYS NEED TO BE THE BEST.

We all want to have a good reputation with our friends and family. Also, we want to be the best person in the world and not phony.

Most people want to be cool for your friends and the people who love you. You don't want to let them down.

You feel always feel pressure from your family, especially your parents. You don't want them to be disappointed in you. You also feel the same way about how your teacher feels. Personally, I feel I put too much pressure on myself to be perfect.

You feel that by being the best you will have more friends even though it is not a good way to get friends. Some friends like to pretend you are friends but they should love you and want you as a friend for who you are.

People just tell you that you have to be better, but you can be what you want to be. You can be better or best.

We all have an ability to be the best, that's why we strive for it so much. Perfectionism is in all of us. It might not be a bad idea to stand back sometimes and let others get a chance of being the best.

Being motivated to be **your** best is a good thing. It is okay to want good things for yourself and to work hard to achieve your goals. But remember, you don't have to be the best at everything. You just must be your best self. Give yourself a break.

BY KHADIJAH ROUINE

26

I WONDER WHY I SOMETIMES DON'T LIKE MYSELF.

I'm used to seeing social media and finding people who all look great and are doing amazing things. This makes me feel like I am not good looking and do not have a nice body because I am a little heavy. It seems like everything I see on TV and on social media wants me to be perfect. I try to accept that I am human and not like these images I tend to see all the time. Sometimes other kids do not say nice things about me which makes me feel bad. I need to learn to be tougher and not judge myself by what I see on social media or TV.

I often see things that make me feel uncomfortable, unsafe, or that give me anxiety. Our school had some people come to talk to the kids about being safe online. They said that when you see something bad on the internet, you should "Stop, Block, and Talk", which means stop looking at the site, block it on the computer, and talk to someone right away about what you saw or heard online that made you upset.

When you see something online that upsets you, follow the directions to "Stop, Block, and Talk." Tell your teacher or your parents that you have seen and heard something on the internet that has upset you. Then you can talk about it. it's not a good idea to keep this to yourself. Maybe it is hurting someone else, too.

Sometimes you feel disappointed in yourself. You may not get the grade you were expecting or perhaps someone said something mean about you that you start to believe is true. Turn to friends who know you and like you for who you are. They can encourage you. Find things you do like about being "you" and remember those things especially during these times.

27

 # TIME TO WONDER

I WONDER WHY I FEEL SO ALONE BEFORE I GO TO BED.

Maybe you feel alone because you miss someone who you always hangout with like friends and family. Being with people all day is fun and sometimes when you are home alone you feel very alone.

WRITE YOUR THOUGHTS

DOODLE YOUR THOUGHTS

28

I WONDER WHY I HAVE SO MUCH TROUBLE MAKING DECISIONS.

I WONDER WHY SO FEW PEOPLE CAN RELATE TO HOW I THINK.

I WONDER WHY PEOPLE PUT SO MUCH PRESSURE ON THEMSELVES WHEN THEY DO NOT NEED TO.

I WONDER WHY WE HAVE FEARS AND ANXIETY.

I WONDER WHY I THINK ABOUT DYING AND WHAT WILL HAPPEN TO ME?

I WONDER WHY I HAVE SO MUCH TROUBLE MAKING DECISIONS.

I find myself overthinking things all the time and then I get stuck. I think you have trouble making decisions because you feel they are very important. You need to make choices and really cannot have it both ways. Sometimes you just do not know the better choice. I guess you learn this as you get older.

Life has so many challenges and it is really hard to get things right. Some decisions are hard and do not have easy choices. That gets you anxious about the choices.

Adults have a difficult time with making choices, too. Two important things about decision making are that a person learns from mistakes that they make when a decision turns out to be incorrect and that a person takes responsibility for decisions that they make. No one selects the perfect choice all of the time. When you make a mistake, forgive yourself, learn from the consequences, and try better the next time.

Making decisions is a big part of growing up. However, it can be scary because when we make our OWN decisions, we must live with the consequences. When your parent or teacher makes your decision, you don't feel responsible for that decision. When you make your own decisions, you will start to feel powerful and that you are in control of your life. It is a good feeling!

I WONDER WHY SO FEW PEOPLE CAN RELATE TO HOW I THINK.

How you think is what makes you unique from others in your way of thinking. You should voice your opinion more so that others may also relate to what and how you think. By doing this, maybe you can learn from how others think, too.

I WONDER WHY PEOPLE PUT SO MUCH PRESSURE ON THEMSELVES WHEN THEY DO NOT NEED TO.

When we put too much pressure on ourselves, we become stressed and not perfect. Sometimes we want to be perfect, even if we don't have to.

A lot of the time you are the one putting pressure on yourself. You might think your parents would feel disappointed in you if you did not do well in school, but that is very rarely the case.

I WONDER WHY WE HAVE FEARS AND ANXIETY.

We have fears and anxiety because our body and mind get uncomfortable and we don't think clearly. We begin to think we are going to fail or not perform up to our expectations. We sometimes get scared and do not think clearly. We cause this to happen to ourselves and make ourselves crazy. Most of us bring anxiety on ourselves. We need to learn to relax and not think we have to be great all the time.

I WONDER WHY I THINK ABOUT DYING AND WHAT WILL HAPPEN TO ME?

It's natural to think about dying. After all, no one lives forever. Talk about how you feel with your friends and family. Don't spend too much time thinking about dying. Get busy living!

YOUR TURN

> I wonder why accomplishments feel so good.
> I wonder why I feel more pressure to do well in school than my friends.

YOUR TURN

*I wonder why sometimes I feel like I do not belong.
I wonder how I will be remembered by others.*

BY JULIETTE ALVAREZ

34

CHAPTER FOUR
UNDERSTANDING OTHERS

I WONDER WHY SOME PEOPLE ARE NICE AND OTHERS ARE MEAN.

I WONDER WHY SOME PEOPLE ARE SHY.

I WONDER WHY NEW KIDS FEEL LEFT OUT.

I WONDER WHY KIDS THINK SO DIFFERENTLY THAN ADULTS.

I WONDER WHY I AM NOT GOOD AT UNDERSTANDING HOW OR IF I HAVE HURT OTHER PEOPLE'S FEELINGS.

I WONDER WHY SOME PEOPLE ARE NICE AND OTHERS ARE MEAN.

Some people might be nice and some might be mean. The mean people might be having a bad day, having sad things happening at home, or having a fight with a friend. They are probably taking it out on others because they do not know how to handle it and are really sad. It doesn't mean they are not nice.

They might have something going on in their lives that feels hard to manage. When people carry around emotions and unprocessed trauma, it builds up. The weight of this can come out as mean behaviors.

I WONDER WHY SOME PEOPLE ARE SHY.

Sometimes our emotions are messing with your head which makes you not want to talk to people. If you can try to just say what you are thinking at the moment and get a positive response from others, you might get over being shy.

Some people may not like to socialize. They might think that they are weird so then they try to stay away from people. Shy people might not like having people look at them and ask them questions.

It is not easy for everyone to be outgoing. Shy people sometimes want to be a part of things but are afraid that they might not be accepted or that someone will judge them. If you see a person who seems to be shy, try inviting them to participate and help to give them confidence. If you are a shy person, try occasionally to be a part of things. You will be glad you did!

I WONDER WHY NEW KIDS FEEL LEFT OUT.

When kids are new, they don't know what to do to fit in with others. When a new kid comes to a new school, the students should be nice and ask them to join them at lunch or at the playground.

It's hard being the new kid. You worry if you will fit in. Friendships have already been formed and others may not want a new person in your circle. This may make being new even harder. Put yourself in the new kid's place. How would you feel? What can you do to help the new kid feel more comfortable?

I WONDER WHY KIDS THINK SO DIFFERENTLY THAN ADULTS.

Adults usually have more knowledge and experience than kids. Adults can use bigger vocabulary words and have a better understanding of the world around us. Adults can answer questions with different knowledge that kids might not have yet.

Kids think so differently than adults because kids' brains are still developing.

I WONDER WHY I AM NOT GOOD AT UNDERSTANDING HOW OR IF I HAVE HURT OTHER PEOPLE'S FEELINGS.

When other people get their feelings hurt, they may not want to talk about it because they are mad at you or because they are hurt. Sometimes it is hard for me to know when I hurt others' feelings (or) hurt other people's feelings. I wish they would tell me, but most of time they just ignore me.

 # TIME TO WONDER

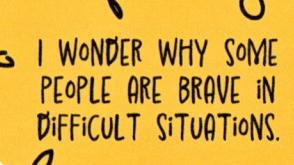
I WONDER WHY SOME PEOPLE ARE BRAVE IN DIFFICULT SITUATIONS.

This is difficult to know. Actually, being brave may be because they have had previous experience in that situation. Maybe they do not fear getting hurt or maybe they always want to help people. I think we all want to be brave but do not know how.

WRITE YOUR THOUGHTS

DOODLE YOUR THOUGHTS

I WONDER WHY SOME TEACHERS ARE MEAN AND OTHERS ARE NICE.

I WONDER IF RUDE PEOPLE ARE REALLY KIND DEEP DOWN INSIDE.

I WONDER WHY SOME KIDS WHO ARE IN THE OLDEST GRADE IN OUR SCHOOL TREAT THE YOUNGER KIDS BADLY.

I WONDER WHY SOME OLDER KIDS THINK IT IS IMMATURE OR UNINTELLIGENT TO KEEP A JOURNAL OR A DIARY TO SHOW YOUR FEELINGS.

I WONDER WHY SOME TEACHERS ARE MEAN AND OTHERS ARE NICE.

When my teacher doesn't call on me when I have my hand raised a lot, I think she doesn't like me. She knows that I probably know the answer. Maybe she wants to give other kids a chance to answer even if they won't have the right answer.

Being a mean and too strict teacher usually makes kids feel more depressed and so the kids act rudely. Bad teaching means that the teacher yells too much, which makes the kids feel guilty and then they act even worse. Kids behave more if their teachers are nicer. This helps kids. If kids like a teacher, they won't take out their anger because they feel more comfortable.

I WONDER IF RUDE PEOPLE ARE REALLY KIND DEEP DOWN INSIDE.

It's rare if a person is truly unkind deep down inside. Most of the time it is what a person experiences that shapes who they are and who they become. Sometimes rudeness can be interpreted by others as being mean. Acting in a rude way may just happen because a person really doesn't know how to behave appropriately.

Unfortunately, rude people either lost their way or they never have been exposed to kindness. Either way it's hard for them to be kind and accept kind actions. Or maybe rude people are not rude; they just speak their minds and others may not like that as well.

BY ALEJANDRA JIMENEZ

40

I WONDER WHY SOME KIDS WHO ARE IN THE OLDEST GRADE IN OUR SCHOOL TREAT THE YOUNGER KIDS BADLY.

My friend's older brother is now in the oldest grade in our school. He makes fun of us, won't play with us like he used to, and tries to act so cool. He used to be our friend, someone who we trusted. We know that he is thinking about how things will be in the new school where he will be the youngest there. We hope that he can be a better role model for us.

Students who are in the oldest grade in a school are getting ready for more serious academic work and often are thinking about their future lives in a way that younger students in a school cannot imagine. Be patient and understand that older students still care about you but are dealing with personal stress sometimes.

I WONDER WHY SOME OLDER KIDS THINK IT IS IMMATURE OR UNINTELLIGENT TO KEEP A JOURNAL OR A DIARY TO SHOW YOUR FEELINGS.

When a kid in an older grade heard that we were keeping journals in our class, he thought that was babyish and silly. Our teacher told us that it is a good idea to let your thoughts and feelings out on paper in your own, private way. That is what we are doing.

Your teacher is giving you great advice. Your journal or diary can be kept very private or used in a way that a wise and trusted adult can help you. Perhaps the older kids are afraid to write down their feelings or confront their positive and negative emotions. Perhaps they don't have someone to go to whom they trust to help them. If you know the older kid well, encourage them to write things down and share them with someone who can help.

41

YOUR TURN

I wonder why people keep hurting others
and do not think they are wrong?

YOUR TURN

I wonder if others see me as a good or bad person?
I wonder why people are mean to others.

BY GENEVIEVE BONAR

CHAPTER FIVE
UNDERSTANDING FRIENDS AND BUILDING FRIENDSHIPS

I WONDER WHY IT IS SO HARD TO MAKE FRIENDS.

I WONDER WHY I SOMETIMES DO NOT WANT TO BE WITH MY FRIENDS.

I WONDER WHY iT iS So HARD To MAKE FRiENDS.

Often it's because you might not know who they truly are and you don't know what other people are like. You also do not know what they like to do and what their interests are. I know it is important to make friends with people who are different than I am.

Because you don't know what other people are like, you are afraid to be rejected. I am also shy and I do not communicate well all the time.

Making new friends can be very challenging when you are not sure others want to be friends with you. They could be mean and hurt your feelings.

Because I am not comfortable around new people I do not know, it is hard to make new friends.. I wish I wasn't so shy. My life would be so much easier.

Sometimes I am afraid if I reach out to others because I fear that I will be rejected and they won't want to be friends with me. That makes me very sad. I need to try harder.

You have to be brave to make friends. You tell people about yourself and it's scary because they may not like the real you. We all want to be liked and make friends, but a real friend will like you for who you are.

It is hard to make new friends. You may feel comfortable with the friends you already have in your circle, but sometimes it is nice to expand your circle. Sometimes it is as easy as smiling and saying hello, and sometimes all it takes is to start a conversation. Try asking a new friend a question about them or ask if they would like to do something or play a game with you. You'd be surprised how easy it is once you get started!

I WONDER WHY I SOMETIMES DO NOT WANT TO BE WITH MY FRIENDS.

Sometimes I just want to be alone and think by myself. Also, when my friends get moody, they make me sad and angry. I need to better understand why they get this way and learn how to better handle it.

When my friends get mean or aggressive, I'd rather be by myself for a few minutes to cool down. Sometimes this feeling lasts for a few days. It feels good to be alone at times, but I need to learn to communicate better.

Some of my friends like to comfort me and then I feel sad that I need help from them. I need to learn to be more accepting of people wanting to help me or be with me.

Of course, we all love our friends, but sometimes we need a break. Sometimes you just need to be alone to have time to think and listen to your own thoughts. It doesn't mean you don't like your friends. In fact, if you take time to take care of yourself, you will be an even better friend!

BY SAHARA JACKSON

47

 # TIME TO WONDER

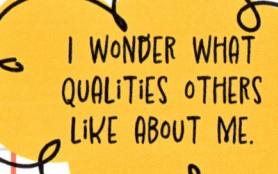
I WONDER WHAT QUALITIES OTHERS LIKE ABOUT ME.

Good question! Think about the things you like about yourself. When you see all of your good qualities, those are the things that other people like about you too!

WRITE YOUR THOUGHTS

DOODLE YOUR THOUGHTS

I WONDER WHY PEOPLE BULLY OTHERS.

I WONDER WHY SOMETIMES I FEEL EXCLUDED BY MY FRIENDS.

I WONDER WHY I FEEL LIKE I NEED TO HELP EVERYONE ELSE.

I WONDER WHY PEOPLE BULLY OTHERS.

I think people bully each other because they think that judging and making fun of them is a cool thing. They probably do not feel they are too cool and so they bully other people.

People bully others because they feel down about themselves. They create another personality for themselves and get mean and rude. I do not think all bullies want to be bullies.

People who bully people might have emotions inside that make them feel weird or different, so they take it out on other people. These bullies feel bad inside and probably are unhappy and have a need take it out on others.

Bullies are jealous of you for the way you look and the friends you have. They really want to be more like you, so they do bad things to get attention from others. Sometimes I just want them to talk to me and let me show them we can be friends.

Bullies haven't learned a lot. They feel bad about themselves or don't care about not becoming better. They may be depressed or there's something bad going on in their lives and they need to get their anger out. It's just school. What's the worst that can happen?

Our school makes a big deal about the ideas of being "kind, safe, and responsible."

People bully other people to make them feel better about themselves. Maybe there is someone who is putting them down or making them feel less than others and by projecting that pain onto someone else it's easier than dealing with their own pain.

People who bully others may have been bullied themselves or are being bullied right now. That does not make it okay. When someone is a bully, they might need help from a trusted adult or a good friend. When someone is hurting, they often try to make themselves feel better by hurting someone else. If you see someone who is a bully, maybe let an adult know so that the adult can get them the help that they need.

I WONDER WHY SOMETIMES I FEEL EXCLUDED BY MY FRIENDS.

Sometimes your friends just want to do something without you. You must learn to better understand them and that they like to be with others sometimes.

Sometimes you feel excluded by your friends because you don't know how to join in. They might think you are unfriendly or snooty.

Sometimes you need to put yourself out there more. Start inviting your friends to do stuff with you so you can become closer with them. They probably want you to reach out more and show an interest in them.

I WONDER WHY I FEEL LIKE I NEED TO HELP EVERYONE ELSE.

I want to feel needed and for people to acknowledge me and to think I am a good person.

I need to feel valued and want to listen to my ideas.

YOUR TURN

I wonder if my friends will leave me for other friends.
I wonder if I really want to lean on others or have them lean on me?

YOUR TURN

I wonder why I have a strong need to feel valued.
I wonder if my friends know who really I am?

BY ANNA WU

CHAPTER SIX
FAMILY RELATIONSHIPS

I WONDER WHY FAMILIES ARE SO IMPORTANT.

I WONDER WHY IT HURTS SO MUCH TO LOSE A LOVED ONE.

I WONDER WHAT MAKES PEOPLE LOVE EACH OTHER.

I WONDER WHY SOME OF MY FRIENDS HAVE TWO MOMS OR TWO DADS.

I WONDER WHY FAMILIES ARE SO IMPORTANT.

A family makes you feel not alone and not lonely. They are your best friends especially when you need them the most. They are the people who will always love you and that will always be at your side.

Family is everything - You need special people around you to feel love that is unconditional.

I think families are important because they mold who we are as a person. They are our legacy! They help us to identify who we are and why we are the way we are.

I WONDER WHY IT HURTS SO MUCH TO LOSE A LOVED ONE.

Because when you get really attached to that person you never want to leave them, so when they leave it hurts because you feel loved and safe.

Because I get attached to people who care about me. I get used to the feeling of being loved and cared for so when I lose someone I really hurt. I get sad they are not on my side anymore.

Because I really trust them and love them with all my heart and it is hard to let go.

Our lost ones usually help us through tough times. When they are gone, it's so much harder to get through challenges. You've lost your support system.

It is unfair when you lose a special pet, like your dog, who has been in your entire life and other people don't understand why you are sad or depressed about it. A pet is a big part of our family. It is a loved one, too.

Perhaps that person shaped/influenced you when you needed it the most. Knowing you won't see them again makes you crave them even more. Knowing they are no longer with you makes a deep void in your life.

When you lose a loved one it can feel like your heart is broken. It hurts because you will miss being around that person so much. Remember that a person is still with you when you take time to remember them and think about them. If you keep the memory, they will always be with you.

I think the idea that someone is there one day and then they are not, is so hard for the brain to process. The permanence of not being able to have one more phone call or make one more memory with that person creates an immense amount of sadness.

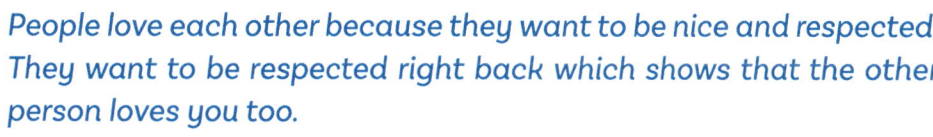

I WONDER WHAT MAKES PEOPLE LOVE EACH OTHER.

People love each other because they want to be nice and respected. They want to be respected right back which shows that the other person loves you too.

People love others because they like to help other people, like being kind and love to be loved back. You want to support each other and spend time together making each other's life better. I think it is something magical and just happens.

I WONDER WHY SOME OF MY FRIENDS HAVE TWO MOMS OR TWO DADS.

There are all kinds of families. Some kids have no mom or no dad at all for different reasons. Some kids have things called step families which means they have more than one person called mom or dad and maybe many step brothers and sisters. And in some families, kids have two moms who are married to each other or two dads who are married to each other. The best part is that all these parents love their kids and build families of love.

Love is love no matter what. Families come in all shapes and sizes. Anyone that loves you and helps take care of you is family. Families are lucky when they have people who love each other.

BY MAKAIYAH UGDAH

 # TIME TO WONDER

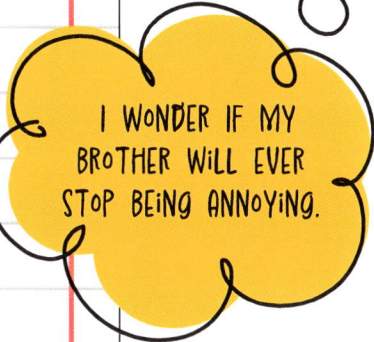

I WONDER IF MY BROTHER WILL EVER STOP BEING ANNOYING.

My younger brothers are so annoying. They bother me too much. I love them but at points I'm so tired of them bothering me. I can't wait for them to grow up and start not being annoying at times.

Probably not! But that doesn't mean he doesn't love you. Find something you both have in common and he'll be less annoying.

WRITE YOUR THOUGHTS

DOODLE YOUR THOUGHTS

YOUR TURN

I wonder If my dad ever thinks about me.
I wonder if I will love someone other than my family.

YOUR TURN

I wonder if my family has secrets they are keeping from me.

BY SABIHA RAHMAN

62

CHAPTER SEVEN
CONNECTING WITH YOUR PARENTS OR OTHER ADULTS IN YOUR LIFE

I WONDER WHY MY PARENTS TREAT ME LIKE A CHILD ALL THE TIME AND DO NOT TRUST ME WITH IMPORTANT TOPICS?

I WONDER WHY MY PARENTS DO NOT TRUST ME.

I WONDER WHY I CANNOT TALK TO MY PARENTS ABOUT SERIOUS MATTERS.

I WONDER WHY MY PARENTS TREAT ME LIKE A CHILD ALL THE TIME AND DO NOT TRUST ME WITH IMPORTANT TOPICS?

Because sometimes I'm not responsible or mature.

I do not think my parents realize I am getting older and able to talk about important things. Sometimes they don't ask me opinions about things that I think I know something about. Some of my friends feel the same way.

Your parents might be trying to protect you. Even if you think you should be included and can handle it, they don't want you to have to deal with it.

It's because for them it's very hard to assume their child has grown and to protect you.

It is hard for parents to let their kids grow up. Show your parents with your actions that you are ready for more responsibility like a grown up. When they see you acting more grown up and being more responsible, they will not treat you like a child anymore.

I WONDER WHY MY PARENTS DO NOT TRUST ME.

I think that they don't trust what you say because I have lied before about things and so they just don't listen to me.

If you lie too many times, your parents will not trust you. You need to learn how to be honest and give them time to change how they feel about you.

Be honest. Have you given them a reason not to trust you? Communication and trust go hand in hand. Being true to your word and keeping your promises will help build trust.

I WONDER WHY I CANNOT TALK TO MY PARENTS ABOUT SERIOUS MATTERS.

I don't tell them the serious matters because I feel like they are going to judge me and think my decision making is bad.

Because sometimes I'm scared of how they're going to react. They do not really listen. They are always doing something else when I try to talk to them.

If you are embarrassed and don't want to talk to your parents or can't talk to you parents, it is good to have a special grown-up in your school to talk to. Let the kids in the school know about this person and that the person is ready to listen to kids privately. That way, kids will understand that they can talk about things that bother them and it will be no big deal.

If your parents don't know about a problem or a feeling that you are having, they cannot help you deal with it. Talk to your parents or another adult that you trust like a tutor or school counselor. It always helps.

I would say because you need trust to talk to them and you're worried about them not understanding why or how you feel the way you feel.

Sometimes it seems like parents don't understand what kids are going through. Sometimes they aren't ready for a serious conversation. Don't give up on them! Keep trying to talk and let them know that you understand that the conversation might be difficult.

TIME TO WONDER

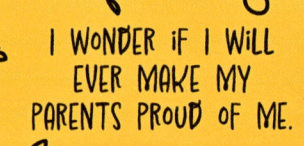
I WONDER IF I WILL EVER MAKE MY PARENTS PROUD OF ME.

I think it's up to you.
You need to give them reasons.

WRITE YOUR THOUGHTS

DOODLE YOUR THOUGHTS

I WONDER WHY OLDER PEOPLE DO NOT ACKNOWLEDGE ME FOR WHAT I THINK ABOUT.

I WONDER WHY I AM CLOSER TO ONE PARENT THAN THE OTHER.

I WONDER IF MY PARENT WHO DOES NOT LIVE WITH ME WORRIES ABOUT ME.

I WONDER WHY OLDER PEOPLE DO NOT ACKNOWLEDGE ME FOR WHAT I THINK ABOUT.

Some older people are set in their ways and find change difficult. Be patient and acknowledge what they've been through. Continue to have conversations that will let your voice be heard.

I WONDER WHY I AM CLOSER TO ONE PARENT THAN THE OTHER.

A lot of the time whichever parent is around more you naturally become closer to them. It does not always mean you love one more than the other. It could be as simple as you just feel more comfortable around one.

I think one parent can be harder on you than the other. You really can't talk to them. The other one can be cooler and easier to talk to than the other.

My dad is always working, but he is always there when report cards are out.

You might be closer to one parent than the other because that parent spends more time with you when it really matters and you create a bond.

Sometimes it's because you have better communication with one of the parents than the other and maybe because you spend more time with one and not the other, you have more trust in one.

Sometimes we worry about this because we think it means we don't love the other parent. You DO love them both, but you might just have more in common with one of your parents or you might have similar personalities.

I WONDER IF MY PARENT WHO DOES NOT LIVE WITH ME WORRIES ABOUT ME.

My father is someone just like me who thinks about things constantly, but it is rare that he shows his worries on the outside.

I think my father worries about me even though we haven't seen each other in a while. I wonder if he is ever going to come back into my life and be a real father to me.

I think dads and moms worry just as much about the child. Parents always try to protect their kids. When you are not with your parents, it's hard for them to keep you protected, so they worry. They worry even if they don't tell you.

BY SAHARA JACKSON

69

 # TIME TO WONDER

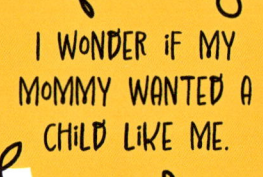
I WONDER IF MY MOMMY WANTED A CHILD LIKE ME.

I think my mommy loves me no matter what and she wanted me.

WRITE YOUR THOUGHTS

DOODLE YOUR THOUGHTS

YOUR TURN

*I wonder if my parents can teach me how to take
care of a child so I can be a good parent.*

*I wonder if my parents really want to know me.
I wonder what my parents talk about at night when I am not around?*

BY NAM NGUYEN

CHAPTER EIGHT
EQUITY, PERSONAL RESPONSIBILITY AND MAKING THE WORLD BETTER

I WONDER WHY SOME PEOPLE ARE LESS FORTUNATE THAN OTHERS.

I WONDER WHY BLACK PEOPLE BELIEVE WHITE PEOPLE ARE MORE IMPORTANT THAN BLACK PEOPLE.

I WONDER WHY EVERYONE IS NOT CREATED EQUAL.

I WONDER WHY SOME PEOPLE ARE LESS FORTUNATE THAN OTHERS.

This is something I've wondered about for many years. I still have not come close to any answers. I sometimes think is all luck depending on where you were born, whether you had two parents, what kind of jobs they have and if they are motivated to work.

I WONDER WHY BLACK PEOPLE BELIEVE WHITE PEOPLE ARE MORE IMPORTANT THAN BLACK PEOPLE.

Everyone said whites are more important than Blacks and whites start to think maybe they were more important than Blacks.

Not everyone who is white thinks this. It is sad that Blacks think this is true. Whites need to learn more about people like Martin Luther King and his supporters. They tried to work for more equality. Many whites helped them.

I WONDER WHY EVERYONE IS NOT CREATED EQUAL.

I've always wondered why most of the bus drivers, custodians, street fixers, and restaurant workers in my neighborhood are usually Black. My mother tried to explain about what still has to happen in our country to make jobs and other things more equal. I'm pretty sure I don't understand what she was trying to explain, but something has to happen to make our country more equal for everyone.

I believe that people have made it this way. We are all beautiful creatures yet others who think they are better, put others down because of their insecurities or their fear of not getting ahead.

*People **are** created equal. However, sometimes people aren't treated equally. People are different and have different abilities and personalities, and we don't always like everyone that we meet, but that doesn't mean that we can treat someone differently. Color of your skin, the language you speak and the neighborhood where you live should not determine whether you are not equal to those who have much more.*

BY ALEJANDRA JIMENEZ

 # TIME TO WONDER

I WONDER WHY I HAVE SO MANY NIGHTMARES.

Because I watch too much scary movies or read too many horror books. I also watch too many violent TV programs.

WRITE YOUR THOUGHTS

DOODLE YOUR THOUGHTS

I WONDER WHY THE WORLD IS UNFAIR.

I WONDER IF THERE IS A HIDDEN WORLD OF PEACE.

I WONDER WHY SOME PEOPLE ARE LUCKIER THAN OTHERS.

I WONDER WHY SOME PEOPLE WANT TO CHANGE THEIR BODY.

I WONDER WHY THE WORLD IS UNFAIR.

I think the world is unfair because the world is just one big circle, and some things need to be good and others bad.

The world is unfair because there are too many problems and we cannot figure out how to help everyone. Usually, the rich people have a better life and those without money always struggle.

It is unfair because we live in a world where people are driven to be better than the next person. We lose sight that we are here together and could be of service by sticking together and lifting one another. Acting on these ideas could end homelessness and poverty,

I WONDER IF THERE IS A HIDDEN WORLD OF PEACE.

We often think that we are living in a dark place with many wars, poverty, and gun violence. We want peace to be able to live safely and with happiness. I'd hope there is a hidden world of peace, if it exists.

I WONDER WHY SOME PEOPLE ARE LUCKIER THAN OTHERS.

I think we notice this because we may not recognize the gifts we have. We take ours for granted and see others' lucky moments as something we will never experience.

I WONDER WHY SOME PEOPLE WANT TO CHANGE THEIR BODY.

Some people want to change their bodies because people say things about their weight, size, and how they look. People are dissatisfied and want to change things.

If you are not the right body type, you are considered not beautiful.

They want to change their body because maybe they're being treated differently or being in a lot of pain. If you are insecure or have been body shamed, you are seeking to change yourself.

The internet shows things that aren't realistic. This often makes people who are insecure or depressed feel ashamed. Some people do not take the time to look at another person except for what they see on the outside. That isn't fair.

It's not just people, it's most of our society. They make us think that our body is not good enough for the world so we must seek changes, even if we do not want them.

YOUR TURN

I wonder if others have the same hopes and dreams I do.

YOUR TURN

BY JAYVIN MENDEZ

82

CHAPTER 9
HOPES AND DREAMS

I WONDER WHY PEOPLE THINK EVERYTHING THEY DREAM WHEN YOU ARE ASLEEP COMES TRUE.

I WONDER WHY DREAMS THAT YOU HAVE WHEN YOU ARE ASLEEP ARE OFTEN SO SCARY.

I WONDER WHY I SOMETIMES ONLY REMEMBER PARTS OF MY DREAMS.

I WONDER IF MY HOPES FOR MY FUTURE HELP ME IN HOW I LIVE MY LIFE.

I WONDER HOW PEOPLE FROM DIFFERENT BACKGROUNDS AFFECT HOW THEY SEE THE WORLD?

83

I WONDER WHY PEOPLE THINK EVERYTHING THEY DREAM WHEN YOU ARE ASLEEP COMES TRUE.

My parents say dreams come true if you dream about something enough times. I am not sure about that but I hope so. I am happy when I remember my good dreams.

A couple nights ago I had a dream of becoming a millionaire and owning my own business and starting a family. The reason this helps me in life is because it shows me that nothing is impossible and to work hard and to NEVER GIVE UP and to always follow my dreams.

I WONDER WHY DREAMS THAT YOU HAVE WHEN YOU ARE ASLEEP ARE OFTEN SO SCARY.

I think your mind plays games and tricks on you and then your dreams get angry. It is upsetting but sometimes my dreams tell me important things like to be careful when crossing the street or follow the rules when swimming.

If a dream is scary, it isn't a dream; it's a nightmare.

When you feel tired, you don't talk much. I try to think about good thoughts when I go to bed and if I find that the bad thoughts are coming into my mind, I switch to things that make me happy.

I WONDER WHY I SOMETIMES ONLY REMEMBER PARTS OF MY DREAMS.

Maybe if forget what I dream because I have many dreams and my brain gets overwhelmed.

When you are sleeping, your brain is resting too. If you wake up at certain times in your sleep cycle, you may not remember anything at all. Sometimes you only remember a few things. If you want to remember more, try keeping a notebook by your bed and when you wake up, jot down what you remember right away.

I WONDER IF MY HOPES FOR MY FUTURE HELPS ME IN HOW I LIVE MY LIFE.

They sometimes do help you in life because they could help you know what you want to be when you grow up. Sometimes you have dreams that inspire you and give you cool ideas about living life.

Some people really think so. Some people are able to remember their hopes for the future and write them down. Then they try to do things that will help them make these hopes come true, like getting the best education that they can.

I WONDER HOW PEOPLE FROM DIFFERENT BACKGROUNDS AFFECT HOW THEY SEE THE WORLD?

It is because we have our own thoughts and so that means we have our own realities and so we dream a lot about things. This makes us different from others and allows us to learn from others.

People grow up in different places and even if someone lives close to someone else, the city might be different than the suburbs or a public school might be different than a private school. Living in a house is different than living in an apartment. Having a big family with a lot of sisters and brothers and cousins is different than being an only child.

BY ALEJANDRA JIMENEZ

 # TIME TO WONDER

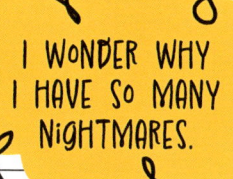 I WONDER WHY I HAVE SO MANY NIGHTMARES.

Because I watch too much scary movies or read too many horror books. I also watch too many violent TV programs.

WRITE YOUR THOUGHTS

DOODLE YOUR THOUGHTS

YOUR TURN

I wonder if others have the same hopes and dreams I do.

YOUR TURN